The Silence...
Between Two Words

The Silence.....
Between Two Words

Dr. Ratikanta Mishra

BLACK EAGLE BOOKS
Dublin, USA | Bhubaneswar, India
2022

BLACK EAGLE BOOKS
USA address:
7464 Wisdom Lane
Dublin, OH 43016

India address:
E/312, Trident Galaxy, Kalinga Nagar,
Bhubaneswar-751003, Odisha, India

E-mail: info@blackeaglebooks.org
Website: www.blackeaglebooks.org

First International Edition Published by
BLACK EAGLE BOOKS, 2022

THE SILENCE... BETWEEN TWO WORDS
by Dr. Ratikanta Mishra

Copyright © **Usha Mishra Mohapatra**

All rights reserved. No part of this publication may be reproduced, stored in a retrieval system, or transmitted, in any form or by any means, electronic, mechanical, photocopying, recording or otherwise without the prior permission of the publisher.

Cover & Interior Design: Ezy's Publication

ISBN- 978-1-64560-277-4 (Paperback)
Library of Congress Control Number: 2022938955

Printed in the United States of America

Dedicated to
> **My Parents**

> My mother inspired me
>> to hold the roots of 'Being'
>
> My father pushed me to the
>> precipice of 'Becoming'

Sri Baikunthanath Mishra, O.E.S.(II)
> Ex. Headmaster,
> Manmath Nath High School,
> Pattamundai, Kendrapara

Mrs. Manju Prava Mishra
> Home maker

Sri Sachidananda Mohapatra, O.A.S. (1) Junior
> Retd. bureaucrat
> Gamu, Bari, Jajpur

Mrs. Radhamani Mohapatra
> Home maker

— **Ratikanta**

FOREWORD

I am that perennial cursed self of 'Vishwakarma' who has not seen the 'Vishnu Pratima' he has sculpted. He might have, but has he had that 'Inner Vision' (antardrishti) to see the darkness of light, know the depth of Eternity. These profound questions beg no answers. There lies the hallowed mystique of these celestial metaphors.

I am that blessed Self of 'Indradyumna' to proclaim with the courage of humility that this temple of poems is not mine.

Poetry loses its poetic echo when the lap of the Mother, nudity of the nude, oozing blood of the wound, angst of the anguish, innocence of the child, trembling lips of the beloved, the fragrance of the flower, the murmur of the bee, dew drops on the grass in an Autumn morning et al are defined in words. Should they be treated in such prosaic way? Can any Poet as such excepting The Great Poet theorise such Poetic concepts of sensibilities?

Where do I stand and what is my identity? I do not know. This is not my humility, believe me, this is the hard truth.

With the wisdom of my beautiful surroundings in view, I dedicate each petal of the flower, each flower of this garland to the critical insight of my readers.

Dr. Ratikanta Mishra

ACKNOWLEDGEMENT

My sincere note and lore of acknowledgement is humbly narrated before you.

You are my loving spouse Usha Mishra Mohapatra and blessed son Ronit (Sipun) to inspire me to pen my thoughts, feelings, anguish and suffering for all these years.

You are my elder brother Er. Saroj K. Mishra, Sister-in-law Mrs. Kabita Tripathy Mishra, nephews Anurag and Anshuman to be my constant source of guidance for a long time since.

You are my elder brother-in-law Dr. Baikunthanath Panda, elder sister Mrs. Nirupama Mishra, nephew Soumya, daughter-in-law Sona who have, all the time been instrumental to expand the horizon of my Creative Persono.

You are my younger brother-in-law Dr. Hrudananda Sahoo, Little Sister Lakshmi, nieces Babli and Bulti, beloved Son-in-law Shailendra and above all my grandson to have considered me to be one amongst you all. I appreciate and honour the creative endeavour of my loving sister.

You are my younger brother-in-law Srikant Mohapatra, sister-in-law Sasmita Mohapatra, lovable niece Aakrit who have played the pivotal role of a catalyst in moving forward the circumference of my joy and happiness.

All my co-brothers Dr. Prakash C. Dash, Prayas Satpathy, Pravat M. Dash, Co-sisters Jyotsna Dash, Sandhya Satpathy, Snigdha Dash and my very dear 'Z', Z plus and millennials young friends Sipra, Sai, Sreya, Sattvic, Subham and above all my grandson Saswat deserve special mention for their love, affection and blessings.

Remarkable as it is so, I remember gratefully the sterling contribution of my younger brother Sri Arvind in shaping my personality and adding a significant meaning to my innermost core.

My note of acknowledgement remains incomplete without the good wishes of my friends, philosophers and guides.

They are :

Prof. Fakir Mohan Sahoo, Research Professor, Xavier University, Bhubaneswar, Dr. Prakash C. Mohapatra, noted Political Scientist, Dr. Aniruddha Panda, a great teacher of Philosophy, Prof. Ramakanta Singh, a literary critic and teacher of English Literature. Dr. Birakishore Dash, a sociologist of repute, Dr. Basant K. Sahni a connoisseur and a Social activist in his own right, Sri Tushar K. Mohanty a bureaucrat with intellectual and professional integrity, Sri Sangram K. Mohapatra, a bureaucrat and an illustrious fiction writer in Odia. Dr. Ranjan K. Sahoo, Associate Professor of Statistics, Gangadhar Meher University, Sambalpur, Dr. Subhas C. Pradhan, Reader in Economics, Biju Patanaik College, Bhubaneswar, Sri Nigamananda Nayak, more an elder brother and reader in History, Indupur College, Kendrapara.

Sri Gagan Bihari Behera, ABDO, Baripada Block, Sri. Manas R. Panigrahi, a banker friend and well-wisher, Mayurbhanj, Sri Manmath K. Patra, Reader in Sociology, Badapada College, Pattamundai, Kendrapara. Sri Sampad

K. Nayak, himself an accomplished creative Persona, in the field of lyrics, short story, poetry and essay, Asst. Manager, D.I.C. Bhawanipatna, Kalahandi. Pradipta K. Sundarray, a Patna based NGO Management Professional. Mrutyunjay Patri, a management strategist of Balasore. Sri Siddharth Pal, younger brother and a cultural activist in Rairangpur, Mayurbhanj. Marut, a Balasore based sculptor and a contemporary cultural critic. Netaji Rath, journalist based in Khunta, Mayurbhanj exteemed colleagues in Khunta, Betnoti, Bijatala and Rairangpur Blocks in Mayurbhanj, Bolagarh and Begunia Blocks in Khordha and all others so dear to me, known as well as unknown.

My dream would not have seen the light of the day without the sincere and painstaking efforts of Sri Satya Patnaik, Director, Black Eagle Books. I express my gratitude to him and his team.

I seek the blessings of Lord Jagannath to pursue this Creative Odyssey to know a little of my
SELF AND BEYOND
LIFE AND AFTER

Ratikanta
Bhubaneswar

CONTENTS

The heaven isn't too far	15
The limited infinity	19
The defined identity	23
The sacred illusion	27
I belong to a continuity	31
The wilted white lilies	35
A detached narcissus	38
Sky - - - The ultimate mystique	40
The cajoled moon	44
The sculpted graveyard	48
The penumbra of flame	51
The other - - - At another end	54
The Invader - - - in search of a mirage	59
The symbolic vacuum	63
On the edge of the precipice	66
The ruined fortress	68
The oozing wound	72
The sublime dust	76
De-meaning the prayer	79
Silhouetted against a void	82
A new millennium - - - on the horizon	86
The atlas is lost - - - somewhere	89
The vacuum - - - within and beyond	91
I'm not - - - the other	94
The elusive deception	96
Battles are half won	100
The linear circle	103
Et tu ! The saviour lumpen	106
The churchyard - - - as seen from the palace	109
The tilt of the axis	112
The sleeve of the conjuror	115
The golden deer	118
'x' and 'n' - - - the grammar of relationship	121
The silence - - - between two words	124

THE HEAVEN ISN'T TOO FAR
[I]

I live in
the recess
    of
  two lives.

    One strangulates
      the other
         liberates.

      An inner link
        establishes communion
          between
          the two.

        I belong
          neither here
            nor
            there.

          The fence
            remains
            as it is.

[II]

A storm
    pervades
the whole sky.

        A loneliness
           embraces
        my whole Being.

                Blissfully
                I' m a lonesome
                    Pilgrim
                  in the midst of
                  a horde of
                      wayfarers.

                            I meet
                            my own
                            'SELF'.

[III]

The chariots move
  on the dusty
    path
  with no Deities
    on board.

      The little child
      in his mother's arms
          cries,
          mocks
        the tourists
        feigning to be
            devotees
            saying

          'I have seen
            GOD
          measuring the distance
          between the palace
              and
            the path
            temple
              and
            the seashore.

[IV]

   The flag atop
      the temple
      and the
   humble waves
      of the
        Ocean
   seem to whisper
      in my ears.

     'The Journey comes
        to an end.
     You don't
        move,
     You are where
        you were
         aeons ago.

     The imprint of
        footsteps is
        somebody else's.

THE LIMITED INFINITY
[I]

Words
spring from
the shivering lips
like the mellifluous
rhythm of flute.
    The rhymes
       of lips
          and
       flute
       converge
       on a point
          where the
              world
          Stands still
            like a
            statue
            waiting for
                LIFE,
            Seeking its
              space.

[II]

The priest is
    nowhere,
only the chanting of
    hymns
pervades the ambience.

[III]

One fateful morning
    a bird
  from the other end
of the flowing stream
    comes
    and whispers
  in the ears of
    the statue

    'I know not
    who am
    'I'.

[IV]

The journey
    begins
on the muddy roads
    and
dirty lanes.
    Sacred and
      profane
    Sublime and
      trivial
      sing
    the same tune.
    'The end is
      seen
    in the womb of
        the beginning.

[V]

Ages later
    the bird
    and
the shadow of
    the statue
        meet
    near a cave of
        Aborigines
       where
    the Inscription reads
        'Man dies,
        words don't.

THE DEFINED IDENTITY
[I]

Close the SKY,
    Open the Ocean
      Add
        not, years
        to
      human lives.
        Break the
        whirlwind of
        Time.

[II]

Atop the
crescent shaped
    hill,
  the priest
in his mundane
    note
    chants
  the hymns of
    ethereal.

    Piercing the
      blue sky
      comes a voice
        with
      divine punctuation.

      'Imprison
      one and all
        o f
      recorded history.
        Etch
      the known texts
      on a piece of
        stone
        lying desolate
        beside the stream.

Bury
all the faceless icons
      of
  yesteryears
on the cemetery of
     memory.

    Retell,
   all the lullabies
     not yet sung
     by a mother
       to her baby.

[III]

Has
each object
    a
    name ?

    Are
    all beings
      gender - specific ?

        Whispers
        a child
        with a questionable
            identity
          to another
              after sunset.

THE SACRED ILLUSION
[I]

In
his courtyard
  the potter
  with moist clay
     makes
   a figurine of
   Divine Angel.

   A piece of
     earth
    gets venerated.

[II]

The azure, blue
    sky
  remains a
    hostage
  to his
    inflated
    male ego.

    The desolate shadow
      of the sky
      dethrones the
        Lady Incarnate
        from her
      holy pedestal.

      The Artiste
        fails
      to compose the
      symphony of
        LOVE.

        The essence of
        Relationship
          gets
        undeciphered.

[III]

On a not so
fateful day of
    December,
a horde of
bigoted clerics
     and
  intolerant devotees
demolished the
     Dome
in Ayodhya
to erect a
saffron flag
    fluttered,
   ironically
    on the same
      apogee
     of the
   Sacred altar
    only to
    find
   at the end
   that the dust
   under the feet
    of the
   Mother-Earth
    remains
    the same
     for you
     and
     me.

The riddle of
    existence
    remains
    unsolved.
The continuum of
    Eternal Questions
    gets
    stretched
Who is greater
    than
        whom,
    God
      or
        Man ?

[IV]

Heavenly bliss
    abound
      when
        we see
          a
            Man in
            a
              GOD.

I BELONG TO A CONTINUITY

Death
has a life,
  Life
has no death.
     Said the Pilgrim
    journeying along
     the banks
       of
      Eternity.

Far,
Far away
the song of Creation
     is
      heard.
    The chorus of
      melancholy
        is
     subsumed
     for the
     Epilogue of
       Tommorrow.

     In the frail twilight
        of
      the day.

the amorous heaven
 surreptitiously
sees the profound nudity
 of
 Mother Earth.

In the grey hours
 thereafter,
the penumbra of
 setting sun
  hugs
the primeval Beings
  to
  her lap
  and
beyond the horizon
 a womb of
  yore,
  fails to
   encapsulate
   the dreams
   of
   the seed.

The seed impregnates
 itself
 gets closer

    to
the Morning Sun
    sees
the revealed intimacy
      of
  He
  and
  She,
in the nearby green
    meadows.
  Listens to the temple
      bells
      and
    murmurs the hymns of
      'LIFE'
  Scribbles the script of
      Identity,
    on the margin of
      existence,
    largely invisible
      to its
    proximate circumference.

      In the nearby
      lotus pond
    of the village
      an old widow
      while offering

'tila tarpan' (obeisance to Sun God)
    sees
the illumined image
        of
        a
        child
        in her
    palmful of water
            and
        feels
            once again
        the ecstatic agony of
            a mother.

        The mother returns
            home
            all alone
            the
            (un)known voice
            resonates,
            vanishes
            into the ether
                atop
                the hillock
                    saying
                'I belong to
                    a
                continuity'.

THE WILTED WHITE LILIES

The deep pond
    has the white lilies
        in
    its embryo

        A few moments
          later,
        the petals of lilies
        blossom into
        native daughters
          o f
        my village.

Daughters are n't
    mere
daughters of yesteryears,
      but
    Goddesses of today
        crying aloud
        the syntax of
            protest
            against oppression
            and
            semingly innocuous of
            not revealing the
            Truth.

The negation of all
　　truths is
　　also
　　the Truth.

　　　Darkness of the
　　Sanctum Sanctotum
　　　　illuminates
　　　the light of the Lion's Gate.

　　　　Near
　　　the century old
　　　desolate temple
　　　　a little girl
　　　　　with
　　　a diya
　　　offers prayer to
　　　the Goddess
　　　praying for the
　　　ascendancy of
　　　　masculinity
　　　to protect one's
　　　　'The Other'.

　　　　The mellifluous stream
　　　　　of the feminine
　　　　flows on the lap of
　　　　　Mother Earth.

Along the stream
  a living corpse
  moves to an
    unknown destination
      and
  far beyond the
clouds
  a living soul
  meditates in
    spatially
  calculated zone.

    Here,
      on a corner of the
        pond,
      the blood oozes
        from the petals
        of the wilted lily.

A DETACHED NARCISSUS

A broken mirror
   shows you,
     your
unbroken / elemental image.
  The image deludes
    you,
  not the mirror
    with
   a wooden frame.

   Within the scarlet
    circumference of your
     native backyard,
      You are you,
       silhouetted against the
        Void.
       touching a small chunk of
        sky.

     You meet your
      identity
     in the constellation of the
      evening sky
      the vengeful light
        melts

in the ember of incandescent
        darkness.

    Each sunrise
       gives a
    new meaning of
         LIFE.
    Your life is
         not
    altogether your
            own.

         It's a
    manuscript of consent
         etched and
         reetched
             by an
         underage prostitute
             sobbing
         in the dead of night.

         You console
             her
         with the everyday
             dictum
         "Life's residues are
             splashed, all across
                 here,
                   there,
                     everywhere.

SKY
THE ULTIMATE MYSTIQUE

Sky,
    a metaphor
  whose deeper aroma
        from
     its navel
      You and
        I
     haven't
     as yet inhaled,
       whose melodious
         cadences
      have evaporated
        into the
      Great Void of
      Cosmos.

     A recurrent
        rhyme
       which,
     the other day
      is the answer
        t o
     an undeciphered text.

A continuum
    a rhythm
      narrates little
        annotates more
          as
          a
        subtext
         in His
        Discourse.

        A Sentence
      with (out) punctuations
          reveals
           the point
     below the exclamation mark
           that
         pushes you
          to an
      uncertain terrain.

      A nuanced idiom
        whose
      subtle messages
          are
         coded
    in the palmleaf manuscripts
          o f
      Pathani Samant
      in the erstwhile

kingdom
   of
  Khandapara.

   A weaved story
      of
    colours
   splashed outside
      the
    canvas of
   Raja Ravi Verma
    that remained
    half made portrait
     of the
    artist himself.

      In a temporal
     momentous timescape
       the sky moves
        eeriely
      along a logical pathway
     to the dark observatory
       o f
    less wise astronomers.

      Here,
      the sky
     afluttered
    over the head of my grandson
      comes

to the lap of my mother
>	to fill up a
missing alphabet
of the lullaby
>	sung by his
>	>	grandmother.
>	Epilogue
>	>	The missing alphabet
>	>	>	is
>	>	the innocence of
>	>	>	the child.

THE CAJOLED MOON

Moon
under her diaphanous veil
    soliloquises,
      You,
    the "Rainbow"
      like an
      intimate enemy
        trespass
      into the Virgin discourse
        o f
    my ancestral lore.

    A soothing touch
      of your clasping lips
        has
    scarred my breast.
    The sign of
    Virgin Mary.
     illuminates
     the sacred
       iridiscence
     among the
      effeminate
      'Yakshas'
      o f
      Heaven.

Said Moon
    to
  the rainbow
    'Come to my
      funeral pyre
       and
      chant all
        profane incantations
        proferring
          for the
        Divine Bliss.

        Wisdom of aeons
          fades,
          wilts
        before the sublime
          black spots
          on my cheeks.

        In the
        Grand Timescape
          o f
          SAMKHYA
          and
          VYAKARAN
          I do
          also, like the transient
            world

    have
three STATES of
    PAST,
    PRESENT, AND
    FUTURE.

      In the Past,
  a secular astronaut
        put
    his feet on
  my supine bosom,
      I was disrobed.

      At present
        the rainbow cajoled me
          t o
        go to Heaven
      with the blemishes of
          A d a m
          and
          Eve.

      In the likely
        far off
          future
        an obstinate child
            i s
          to make me his own

      despite
all the mundane pleasures
      around
        and
      beyond.

           In the imminent dawn
                I
           escape to my,
          'Eternal Void'
            snatching
            the ephemeral joy
              of the child
              with a postscript
                  that
                "I pray to attain
                    evanescent immortality
                    in the little palms
                    of the
                    child.

THE SCULPTED GRAVEYARD

We don't
  choose
where are we to born
    but
  our graveyard
    where
  the rendition of the
      Song of Death
        is
      to be performed
        for the next
          Cycle of Life.

Living corpses
  quarrel
over a piece of land,
  a chunk of sky
  a swanky corner of the
    dejected monument
      but
    dead selves
      find
    a cosy agreement
        to
    narrate the layers of
      RELATIONSHIP.

In the embryo of
    Death
lies the seed of
    Life.

    Death
is the high priest
in the regal ceremony
    of
      Life.

    Life
is a necessary
    appendage
in the surreal
    visage of
    Death.

The sculpted graveyard
    is
the crucible
    where
a Great Dialogue
    ensues
between Life
    and
    Death.
that remains
    inconclusive

to the Day
　　with a
　footnote
　　　'The journey of
　　　　Life
　　　comes to a
　　　geometric end
　　　　with
　　　　Death.

THE PENUMBRA OF FLAME

The black innocent smoke
 of the
cruel flame,
swings up, and up
 in a circular path
  leading to the
   etherscape.

Here,
at an elbow long distance
  lies
a perpetual pregnant
   mermaid
   holding aloft the
   flaming torch
    of
   Creation and
    Destruction.

The vertical smoke
  moving
in a spherical space
   looks back
   and
  finds its chord of
   Identity
  in the rectangular base

Where
the mermaid sees the
horoscope of
Life
and
Death.
Awhile,
the absence of Time
Reigns
in the vacant space.

A little later
an army of apes
are seen
ashore,
collecting crystals
from the conch shells
pebbles are
thrown
into the womb of
the sea.
The sea is
asexual,
effeminate
to be in touch
with
the sand.
In the deep, feminine
evening,
Pebbles are reborn
a n d

crystals become
odourless corpses.
When
night opens the door
to her
'He'
the Penumbra of
flame
engulfs them
both.

THE OTHER - - -
AT ANOTHER END

The lonely sailor
    with his crew
        dies,
everyday,
only to be
    reborn
the next day.
      Today's 'He'
          becomes
      the 'Other'
          tomorrow.

      Waist-deep in
        river,
    the muddied water
      in the Palm of the
        Brahmin
    Upraised in oblation
        t o
      Sun-God
      falls
  in the same river.
    The stream of
      Consciousness
      flows onwards.

Along the bank of
 the Lost River
  a
 cute, dusky
  female
 steps in to the water
  undressed
  murmuring a prayer
   o n
   her lips.
    the revelries of
   the nude body
    continues
    till dawn.
   Nudity
   with all its profane
    sanctities
    be kept
     i n
   a Mystique Box
    under
   the Throne.
    She is a
    harlot,
   known to all
   chics and connoissieurs alike
    people say so,
   Flowing water doesn't.
    On a raft
     sits

a timid man
 with
collateral courage
   and
  the Destiny
    oars it
   to another destination
    he doesn't
     hopefully
      know.

An eagle
   overhead
   descends
to the trunk of the
   uprooted tree
      to
   meet an old dove
     and
    consoles.
   'The better days
    are certain
      to
     come to this
     world
     o f
       ours.

The sailor is
    alive
    and dead
at the same time,
    the undated
    Mariner's Compass
        takes
    the ship
      nowhere.
    Time takes a
        pause
        to
      reinvent itself.
    Years later,
on a summer solstice
          a
      shadowy figure
      becomes visible
        o n
      the sky
      only
      to disappear
          in a
        flickering moment
      becomes
        a speck of dust
          mingled with the
          water.

Man disappears
    but
  the core dust of
    humanity
    remains
  where it has been
    for aeons.

    The sailor reaches
      the gateway to an
    Empire of Occident
        in a
      wintry evening
        and
        speaks
    in a patterned intonation
      " I had seen
      these
      growing apes
        in my
      native land.

    The postscipt
      says
        'I'
      and
        'The other'
          are
            one and
              the same'.

THE INVADER IN SEARCH OF A MIRAGE

The cerebral invader
   from the other end of the
      Caucasian Steppes
         occupies
      the footnotes of History
        to preach the
          sub-text
           that
      closed fists don't nourish
         Relationship.

Lores of
Native Folks
   dig up
long forgotten
     chunks of swamp
        to
      utter
      syntactically
        'Your world
          and
            Mine
           are
              One'.

In the Courtyard
    of
a Temple of
unknown ancestry
   the 'Rajguru'
    in his
   inimitable posture of
    'affirmed dominance'
      eerily measured
     the distance
    between the cracks
     in the crevice
      and
    the summit of the temple.

The folk-tongued
   village priest
     workships
  the antique texts
  and
palmleaf manuscripts
   undeciphered
     to this day yet.

A horde
in their late thirties
    from
  the lush meadows
    along
      the Ganges,
 in
Anglophone intonations
    occupies the

           residual space
                between the
                    twigs and
                        crevices.

Fading alphabets
in 'Devnagari Script
          are
          visible to
              them,
                   the self-esthetes
                        claim so.

The arguments of
          Religious
              and
          Blasphemous
               are scribbled
                    with
                today's signature.

The King
     effeminate and
          much maligned
              in the eyes of
                   his devotees,
in a bizarre
     shade of things
          places
     the Regal Emblem
          with
     the Invader.

The ignominious king
        is
              dead.

The inflated arrogance
        of
        the 'Outsider'
          is
        now an Insider,
        amongst one
          of us
        with the
            prescient grip
                o n
            Past-The King is dethroned,
            Present-Banal history is part of the text.
            Future-Anglophiles are to
                sing eulogies
                    in perpetuity.

Destiny
  has met
    the Oasis
      but
        the sublime mirage
          eludes
            The 'Being'
            and
                The 'Becoming'.

THE SYMBOLIC VACUUM

In a Carnivalesque Silence
   People in hordes
     celebrate ecstatic
       suffering
    on the suburbs,
      lisps the
     poetics of
        violent love
       and
      tender hatred.

"The nuanced edition
     of
fragile innocence
    fails
to draw the alphabet of
     a tale".
    The courtesans of the King
       Proclaim.

"Hyperboles
   from the Throne
    are the
    Papal Sermons
     for the
    subjects in perpetuity".

    Ordered the King
     in his
    authorial voice.
The danse macabre

             of the
       Skeletons on the streets
             with
         the sonorous lyrics of
         hunger, thirst and
             cruelty of Fate,
                eulogise
         the destined 'Raj Dharma'
             of their King.

         The Power brokers derive
             vicarious pleasure
             for their Master.

After
years of Pilgrimage
         returns
       The Great Slave
             to his
         castle of slavery
             and
         offer sweat and blood
                t o
           preserve the illusory
             construct of Power.

The lowly commoners
         half bent
       submit to the
             Saviour
       "we are content
             with our
         joy of desperation,

                    subtlety of hunger
                A sin
            we consider
                to resist
                His Majesty

                    We have mortgaged
                        t h e
                    ammunition to blow up
                        this magnificent
                            Castle of Slavery.

O Divine Incarnation
            we all need
                a cup of
            Socratic hemlock
                    for the last
                    thin veneer
                        o f
                    Protest.

<u>Appendix</u>
                when
            does the King
            care to listen
                to the child
                    who says
                'The Throne is
                        but
                    a speck of dust'.

ON THE EDGE OF PRECIPICE

Waxing
audacious eloquence
   the devotee
   while offering
   an earthen lamp
      with
     a dim flicker
      questioned the
      Deity's
     Existential diffidence.

    The Deity
      meditatively
      in a sculpturesque mood
        remained
        silent.

        Spiritually enervated
          but
        religiously buoyant
           Man
        like all fallen species
          fails to
          evolve from
           within.

Theorem
    He seeks the perennial answer
        outside Himself.

He,
but rarely
talks to
    himself.
The lexical meaning
    of his questions
    sabotage
    the beauty of the
        Inner self.

Deduction
    The subject is
        metamorphosed
          into an object
            of
        neuter gender.

God
exists
in the winter dew drops
    on the grass
    whose
    profundity
and banality
    merge
        in a point.

THE RUINED FORTRESS

After a long
    sojourn
on the holy bank
      of
    Bhagirathi
    with a
    courtesan
      of
impeccable denominations.

    The Emperor is
      back
  to his Courtyard of
      Authority.

Come on
skeletal remains
    of the graveyard
      and
    join the refrain of the
      Royal Prayer
    "Long live
      O' Father
        we offer our
        sweat
          and blood

as Your due
   generations together.
         O'
   The Honour,
   The Saviour,
   The Victor,
   the smudge of blood
           o n
        your elbow
              is
              your
           ancestral property, a piece of
           azure sky
                 i s
           yours, exclusively

              Yours also
                 i s
              the pillar on the
                 vanquished land
                       with
                 undated scribble
                       o f
                 your forefathers
                 on the margin of
                 'Tamra Patra'.

                    We have
                       ours,
                          blazing tide of

hunger,
    unquenched thirst
        dissipated aspirations
            rich foliage of
                desperation
            meaningful innuendos of our
                Hoary Tradition.

        The inchoate gaiety
                of
            Today's festival
            is rehearsed
                atop
            the hillock of
            Pataliputra.

        When the
            translucent
        bluish saree
        of the Mermaid
        of the Ganges
            aflutter
        over the head of
            the king's
            Destiny.

            The Oracle
                of Delphi
                in a
                    didactically morphed tone

                declares
The footprints of the
        courtesan
            along
            the banks of
                    Bhagirathi
            the Mermaid of the
                        Ganges
                and
                the sheenless
                sword of the King
                    are
                fallible engravings
                    o n
                the ruins of
                    Nalanda.

The fate of
        all
    are tremulous
        like
            water
    on a lotus leaf.
            The same bier is
            made ready
                both
                    for the King
                    and
                        the harlot
                        alike.

THE OOZING WOUND

In a corner
　　of the parched wetlands of the
　　　　Savannah,
　　　History
　　stands like a
　　　young widow
　　consciously concealing her
　　　　　wounds
　　　　of awful wrongs
　　　　　　and
　　　　paternal depredation
　　　　　down the times.

　　　Ironically true
　　　　　and
　　　Pedantically theorised
　　　　　History
　　with her stretched fecundity
　　　gives birth to them all
　　　patricians, plebeians
　　　　　alike.

　　　But,
　　　　in a calculated twist
　　　　　of sorts
　　　　　　she is made

to imprison herself,
  to isolate herself
    behind
      the sculpted woodframe
        of
          the Headman.
            She is
              put in a category
                she is
                  unaware of

The wider space
  of
    Sabarimala
      is denied to her.
        She is
          lost in a
            bizarre cobwebs
              of
                Demagogue Patricians.
              The Earth is
            theirs,
          so also is
              the overcast Sky.

The red blood
  splashed on the
    suburbs, bylanes, shanties
      are not

well-manicured
  alphabets
    but
      slashes
        within the brackets.

The Dominant
  and
    the Dominated
      are n't
        same constructs.
          History
            alludes to
              this interpretation.

The native folks
  are
    to shed blood
      and
        History is rewritten
          and
            the Flags of Victors
              are
                unfurled
                  on the cliff of the
                    distant mountain.

Stories
  of all hues
    are
to be yarned
  for
    the Connoisseurs of Power

and
   pages of patriarchy
      on
         humanity
            are to be
               proffered
                  to the
                     inchoate minds of
                        Tomorrow.

On a corner
   of the grasslands
      lie
         ash-filled urn
            to be given
               a
                  formal obeisance,
                     on the banks of
                        the river.

Obituaries are penned
   and
      forgotten
         But
            the lustre
               of the sword
                  remains
                     brighter
                        as ever.

THE SUBLIME DUST

   You
are made up of
      dust,
  shall ye return to the
      dust.
   Identity is born,
    reborn
     and
      lost.

On my journey
     to
   the Courtyard of
     Death,
   the Path of reincarnation
     leads
  to the mound of
      dust,
       here,
        there,
         everywhere.

The bier,
  the graveyard
    the memorabilia

           all
are morphed
        into
   a sacred altar
           where
           the Divine dust
           illumines
               the
               whole space.

The blazing fire
         of
         'YAGNA'
             makes me see
             Myself and
             beyond.

Am I then
     n't a
         speck of dust
             on the forehead
                 of
                 Dust itself.

Aeons before
         a
         big explosion of
         dust
             made this word
                 of
                 Ours.

   A mellifluous lyric of
     a silent duststorm
        is to write
          its
        Epitaph.

On
the Epitaph is
    written
   "The man of
      today
    tries, in vain
     to measure
    the dimension of
       dust
     without inhaling
      the fragrance
      of dust.

DE-MEANING
THE PRAYER

The meaning itself
    doesn't
know its
   meaning.

Prayer,
   per se is
       a n
   object-specific
   neuter gender.
    It is
   mercifully,
  unaware of
     its
   underlying motif.

The primeval prayer
    i n
syllables of silence
    i s
consecrated in the
     oozing
  amber tears of
    my Mother.

Bluish chunk of the
    S k y

is streaming
   off the brush.
Wild splashes of
     colour
    is
       painted on
         the canvas.

The nonchalant painter
     pauses
     awhile.
This is the
Mystique shadow of
    the Deity
  waiting to be revealed
      and
    escape the agony of
       meaning
       and the ecstasy
          o f
         de-meaning.
After
a brief interlude
     of
some moments,
the rippled lyric
   of the stream
     is born
  out of the womb of
      the mountain.
  A melodious breeze
    wafts through
      the emptiness.

The moss of
    History
in the crevices of
    the hermitage
      recounts
    a forgotten lore.

Under
the scarlet circumference
    of the Sky
    My Mother
      prays
    paens in eloquent verses
      for the
    soothing touch
      of
    Death
    for the celestial
      reincarnation of
    'SELF'.

The premise of
    prayer
is the attainment of
    evanescent immortality.
The angst of
    LORD
    is stealthily put
      in the
    bronze pot of
    ambrosia.

SILHOUETTED AGAINST A VOID

'VOID'
  is the only
    'TRUTH'
  to which
    we all have
        to
     return, someday
    without the
      bondage of
        immortality.

A journey
    of earlier centuries
        with its
     sombre dreams,
     ruby hue of love,
       a Junoesque gesture
          of
       some intimate moments
          and
      unfulfilled promises
        are etched
          on
      the treacherous sands of
          Time.

The sceptre
   of
vanquished victory
    is
  planted in a distant
    neighbouring land.
      The sheath of the
          sword
      lies, somewhere else.

For a long, long
    time since
  the King is
  on a spree of conquest,
      claims the regal dominance on the
      rocky terrain
        and
        plain territory of the
        neighbouring kingdom.

The ever obedient
    slaves
   of his kingdom
   are sighing
   requiem
  for their dead kin,
      out
      to avenge
      the humiliation
      heaped on our
      benevolent king.

The widow
in vacuous tearful eyes
    looks at the bier
        pretending not to see,
        feigning to be happy
            i n
        esctatic agony.

The oozing wound
        of
the common
        is
    a scar
        on the forehead of the
            King.

The colour of the tears
        are the same
        both in the eyes of the
            rustic
        and
        sophisticated.

With
the dawn of a new Century
    on the
    Ceremonial Day of
        Coronation
    the wise sage
        in the court of the

                King
            exhibited
    a soiled page of
                history,
                    of
            Regal genealogy
                inscribed on the
                    Royal Charter,
                        that
                    the King and
                        the slave
                            belong
                        to the same
                            family source.

The Royal Emblem
        moves
            forward,
                arch-like
                    in
                self-atonement.

A NEW MILLENNIUM ON THE HORIZON

Horizon
   is an allegorical construct
         of
   Unity and Peace.

    There,
     out there
       on a
       vernal equinox
         the Earth flowers
           in the symbolic sojourn
            of the Sky,
            the vignettes of
               whispers
              are resonated
               on the beach.

The little crabs
   in the sanddunes
      escape
     within the little innocent
        fingers of the
          child.

Here,
   a bit nearer
      to me,
   the poetics of
      lullaby is
      lost to the
      prosaic calculation of
         Man.

The child
  on the beach
     alas,
  has now become a
     Man'
    on the streets.

In the duel between
  who (subject)
     and
  what (object)
  the rainbow isn't
    coming to the
      lotus,
    the Sky is
     no more
    caressing the
     Mother Earth
      on the horizon.

Waves
on the beach
    don't touch
the feet of the child,
       the butterflies
          are n't
            tickling the
              briars.

Man,
in stead of
taking a pleasant stroll
    on the grassbeds
    of his garden,
       tramples upon
          the dew drops
            o n
          the buds of the
              grass.

Still,
    the New Millennium
          is
       a cornucopia of
        possibilities
       on the rich vistas of
          LIFE.

THE ATLAS IS LOST SOMEWHERE

The Atlas
  is the ultimate
    battleground, where
        You
        and
        I
      fight,
      fight for the
        location of the
          axis of
            Power and
            Pride.

A studious slave has
  one, the obstinate,
    disobedient has none.
      The pages of the
          Atlas
        are given identity
         with the stroke
           of the pencil.
        the stroke of the pencil
        moves, in a calculated
           pattern,
         to speak the language

of the Dominant,
   to malign the
     decrepit castaways
         on
      the shores of
         Time.

The wild,
   bizarre
     inane beauty in
       erasing the lines of
          separation,
       between East, West
       Northern, Southern hemispheres
        latitudinal depth
        longitudinal expanse
          are
       the true allusion
         to
       the aesthetic lore of
         'Vasudheiva kutumbakam
           (The World is one Family)

In the Global Village
     of ours
    denominational specifics
      and
    particularities are
      buried
       in our
         common graveyard.

THE VACUUM WITHIN AND BEYOND

A soiled canvas
    in a corner
  of your orchard
      is in search of an
          Artist.
      The Artist is a
         mere medium
           to paint,
           as the painting
             says what it wants
                to be.

The soft touch
    of the vernal breeze,
    the rich foliage of the
        peepal tree
      the amber grains
         on the cornfields
      the melody of the
         cuckoo in this
         Virgin Vacuum
        haven't
         touched you
           a bit

Poetic sensibility
       is a
     victim of
prosaic mensuration.

The cacophony of
    the matter
      has made the
   cadences of
       buoyant ether
      enervated,
       decrepit
      and
        effeminate.

The cityscape of
   yours, is
dotted with the
   upbraided shadows of
      smoke.
     The harlot of
      modernity
       moves you a
        wee bit.

At the other end
    stands
  a sculpture of a
gracious woman
   in the image of
My Mother
with a vermillion mark of
     aesthetics

      on her forehead
        inviting you all
          to listen to
            stories of
              yore.

She is a
   vacuum
   with lots of
      possibilities and
        promises,
           resolve and
              resolutions,
                  to be explored by you.

Are you to
   despite
   your emptiness ?

I'M NOT THE OTHER

Unedited words
　　make me
　　　and
　　the other
　　　separate and
　　　　put in
　　　　　opposite poles,
　　　　　　bitter tongues
　　　　　　　know
　　　　　　no grammar of
　　　　　　punctuation marks,
　　　　　　　and
　　　　　　interrogate
　　　　　　the pronouns of
　　　　　　　Everyday Life.

An archipelago
　　beyond the shores
　　　　invites
　　the raging waves of the
　　　　　Sea
　　　　in an
　　　unearthly hour
　　　　only to
　　　touch each other
　　　　for some
　　　　　flickering moments.

The story
of the desolate archipelago
       isn't
        mine.
    Mine is a
      monument of
      treacherous stone
       and
      innocent moss.

Nonchalant apathy of
     here and
       there,
      now and
        tomorrow
      are the
    horizontal geometry of
         m y
        vertical ignorance.

Bracketed
  as I am
  living in the immediate
     neighbourhood of
       'The Other'
      not to allow
        any sculptor
          t o
        the monument of my
        designed negligence.

THE ELUSIVE DECEPTION

I deceive
   myself
as has always been
   since I
   see an 'I'
     in
      myself.

Over the clouds
   ashore,
in an Autumn afternoon
   I guess
   I'm
   higher and
     bigger than
     those, below the
      Sky,
     higher you go
     humbler you feel
      height is a
       cognate object.
       Stature is the
        determinant.

The distance of moon
    from the
Earth, remains
  always the same.
    My Fifth Floor Avenue
      is no

                    nearer to moon
                        than the
                    vendor on the
                            streets.

Aspiration,
with the innocence of a
            child,
        not
        the vanity
        of the Fifth Floor
            is the pathway
                to moon,
            elevated spirit
                makes you
                    there.

The robes of
   Archimedes
      on that day
      made all
         Athenians disrobed
                  naked,
               he sought,
               unravelled
                  the riddle of
   TIME.
Silk clad
   village head
   called him
         insane.
      Sanity,

        however
          eludes the
            chieftain.

Awoke Alexander
  from a deep
    slumber
    found the crown,
      on the ground,
      tattered and
        dusty.
        ignominious chic.

The sceptre awfully
    melts
  in the residues of
      History.
    A footnote and
        an epilogue are
          added later.

All the alphabets
    of your
  academic calendar
      get blurred when you
      fail to decipher
      the stroke of marks
        between
the lines.
  the blank space
      between
    the lines
      is the

            navel of
                wisdom
                down the times.

The point of
   full stop
        and
   the exclamation marks
        are n't
        the same
            as I had once
                boastfully proclaimed.
                    The point of Full Stop
                            i s
                        the end,
                        the point of
                            exclamation mark
                                prods you,
                                inspires you
                                    t o
                                see beyond.

My conceits
   are mine
   I don't
       lend them to
           anyone.

BATTLES ARE HALF WON

Had
Sage Vyasa
   foretold
    in
  his Original Text
    the
    Ascent of Pandavas
     in corporeal form
       t o
     the cherished Heaven ?

  Hadn't
   the wise man
    annotated
    in a lyrical form
    the duties of
     'Rajdharma'
     of the Victor
      in the Great War of
       Mahabharat ?

  Hadn't
  the Great Conjuror of
    the Age
   kept up his sleeve
     the 'Zeitgeist' of
the contemporary
   'YUGA'

The Kshatriya

    in
obeisance to the clan
      is
  to exterminate the
    Evil Forces and
    Restore
  Pure, Noble Royal Power
      i n
    this 'Aryabhumi'.

Why then
  which is all pre-destined,
  fate takes a different
     course for
  ultimate salvation ?

Half the battle is won
  when the other camp
  is decimated,
    the Other half
    of the battle remains
    as residues of
      Mythology
        a s
    chanting of Vedic hymns
        aren't
  heard
from the sublime anguish
      o f
    the victor
  and The Throne
    doesn't
    step in

       to heal the wounds
             o f
       the Enemies of
         yeaterday.

In a transcript
  added later
'Hastinapur' was
  fated to lie
    forlon,
    orphan
  without
      The First Man.

THE LINEAR CIRCLE

"Achieving nothing
signifying nothing"
   quoted to have been proclaimed
      by the Bard of Avon
        as a charter of
      attitudinal angst of
          humankind
        with the spilt ink
            of mundane arrogance.

On the very same stage
     years later
   T.S. Eliot penned the
     poetic irony
of the beginning in the end
         and
     the end in the embryo of
           beginning.

Here,
along the banks of Gangotri
    the rites and
      rituals and of
     consecration
        and
      desecration
     remain the
        same.

The requiem is a

    mainfesto of
        rebirth
    in a cyclical way.

The bier
that takes dead to the
        graveyard
    is the same
    as the swing of the
        new-born baby,
    a baby,
        in reality
        is reborn
        from the embers of the
            fire.

In a note of
    paraphrase
    we return to the
        same stage
        again and
            again
        till
    the postscript of
        Eternity
            is written,
        the Eternal circle
            moves,
        moves around
            to locate/relocate our
            Destined Path.

There,

there beyond the
Himalayas
    and
across the coast of
    Atlantic
a Straight line
    leads
        to the
            End,
        with a
            signpost
            inscribing the
    Prophetic Proclamation
        "The linear Path
            leads to a
            product of
            numeral equation
                not to be surpassed
                by the poetics of
                    Pilgrim's Journey.

Subtextual Proposition remains thus :
    Contraction of a line
        makes it a
        circle.
    Expansion of the circle
            makes a
            line,
        apparent contradictions
            are
            resolved,
                in the end.

ET TU!
THE SAVIOUR LUMPEN

The Saviour
  of my mother
    in an ironic twist
      of circumstances,
        is a lumpen,
        literate, of course
          but a
            lumpen
              for sure.

The clinical separation
  of the umbilical chord
    from the baby
      to the deformed lap
        and
          abused heart
            is a
      long journey in itself.
      The first cry of the child
        and
          the oozing tears of
            my mother
            are one
                and
            the same voice

emanating from the
  same primeval
    source of
      existential dilemma.

The child
interrogates the surrounding
    and its depth and
      warmth of
        relationship,
          in gay abandon
        He is, however
          not answered

Down
the apogee of
    Time
  the Earth soliloquises
    in a State of
      Solemnity,
    the depth of abyss
      she has been
        pushed into
          albeit
        in a calculated
        manoeuvring way of
            sorts.

  The lumpen
    was not born
      a lumpen.

In those halcyon
    days,
a morsel of food
    was
    enough to
satiate the hunger
    of all.

Today,
    overabundance has made
    most,
    half-fed,
    half-clad
      joy and
        exuberance
      is lost
      somewhere,
    in an unknown corner,
    with the
    concluding index
    being.
    the
pseudo-cerebral manipulation
      t o
    ab (use)
the given reality
    of GOD
to trail blaze
    the legacy of
    irrationality
in the Post-truth
    world.

THE CHURCHYARD AS SEEN FROM THE PALACE

The Oak Tree
    of
an earlier century
    stands, alone
  in the churchyard
   with empty hands
    upraised and
      folded,
     not for its
    outer foliage
      but
    for the long life
     of the roots
       down the earth.

The Oak Tree
  is the
    insignia
     of our
      ancestry.

At the other end
   rose, hibiscus
      Chrysanthemum, lotus
         et al

adorn
   the arch of the
      treacherous palace
         without ever
            tracing the
               logos
                  of their origin.

These,
   beauteous appendages
      blossom and disrobe themselves
         for the bees of
      the neighbourhood
      to be impregnated
         with Pollination.

The Oak Tree
      then
   gives these peerless gifts
         t o
      Earth
      as a mark of
         detachment,
      the tree stands
         sculpturesque
            as before.

The churchyard of
   our ancestors
      was a palace

              once
         in far off
    undated BCE,
              the palace
         with the eternal curse
                   reminisces
                   the day of
              Baisakh Purnima
                   when
                   Tathagata
              abdicates Throne
                        t o
                   become
                        Gautam Buddha.

The palace of
     Shuddhodan
          moves an inch
               towards
                    the churchyard.

THE TILT OF THE AXIS

The tilt of the
    Axis
  favours a few
   privileged,
    connoisseurs,
      elites
    does no favour
     to many
     underlings,
      lumpens
       chics
in the serpentine corridor
     of power.
    where
    man is a unique number
     ration card is
     his horoscope
      absolute
     destined not to
       change
     the smart sarkari
       cards,
     not to be decoded
       anyway,
     can't move
        beyond the

contour lines
    of
      The Establishment.

The Papal Commandment
  "I bow my entire
    mortal body
      over and above
        the overcast Sky
        in their darkly lit
        dungeons of
          Authority,
            they do,
      what they say
          long,
      long before
      the trumpets of the
        Common Man
      are made to blow
    by a watchful eagle
        with
        severed wings.
      Paths to
    Promised Land
      are made
    and unmade
      hearth is burnt
        and
      extinguished
          impure assurance

  are
doled out to
   pure souls.

  I
Perforce forget
  as I have to
   and
    forgive
 in a Christ like manner
  as has been
    my wont.

The miasma of
  their
 Prescient equation
    and
  eerie matrix of
   psychology
  renders the postscript
    apt and
    appropriate
   'Thy Hand
     Great Benevolent'.

THE SLEEVE OF THE CONJUROR

The ace of the
    conjuror
  is a broken toy
    of the child,
  he throws it away
      unnoticed.

The conjuror
    doesn't begin the show
      till the
    tranquil, poised
      slow-tongued adolescent
        occupy
      the front row.

He gets
  upset, nervous
    in the melee
      of the
        subversive
          acid-tongued
            illegitimate underdogs.

The lanky chap
    below 18
    with the conjuror
in his shrill voice
      adores
      his boss
    to be a futurist,

                born out of the womb of
                    an intelligent (Sic)
                        being.

To add
a touch of credibility
            to
    his otherwise fraud acts
        the conjuror, first
            put the authority
                of Establishment
                    under his hammer
                        critiquing
                    the child labour
                    without a wink
                    to his left.

Using the archaic
        text of
    undecipherable alphabets
        the conjuror narrates,
        weaves the web of
            future days,
                the teacher
                    postman
live stock Inspector
    village level worker
    Agriculture field worker
            lift point driver
            a divorce blonde
            a quarrelsome old lady
                    listen
                attentively to

        the concocted
      narratives of
         the conjuror.

Nothing,
    practically nothing
    howsover
    sophisticated the machine may be
        is to remain
    beyond the over-arching limits of
        the villagers,
    the conjuror solemnly
        swears.

Future
enthusiastically beckons
    these adolescents.

There,
  a lumpen
    sees through the
bright hypocrisies
       and
  intelligent chicaneries of the
      conjuror
        and put a hole
      in the black curtain
        of the show.

The conjuror remains
    incognito
      since then.

THE GOLDEN DEER

The deer
in the deep woods of
    Dandakaranya
      like all others
        wasn't a golden deer.

Maithili
  in her bid
  to satiate her
    worldly hunger
      put
    the deer
      in a golden cage.

On the dusty plains
  of this world
    everyone,
    Incarnation of God
      even
    is a prisoner
      of the abbey of
        illusion
        a slave
      of the blandishments
        of
          here
          and
          now.

             became
      merely a pilgrim
           in search of
           a mirage,
          the portait of
             the mirage
                is
                His.
The actors
       we
   ordinary mortals
             see
      on the stage
          are
      in essence and
             elements,
         metaphors that
         escape, vanish
           in the tears of
           the devotees,
                of the
                Idols
           below the Podium.

The demon king
    in the robe of a
             beggar
      is the dejected son
         of the evil
     helplessly waiting
           in the portico
                to
redeem himself

          seeks the redemption
             of his soul,
                the blessings of
                   the Mother
                      he seeks as
                            alms.

Janaki,
from her hut of leaves
   imagines the riches of the
      Golden Lanka
         that radiates
            the false lustre
                  of
   regal arrogance
                  and
      its deceptive cognates.

The trumpet of war
         is the
   Mythological Oracle
      that forewords
         "Everything on the surface
                      glitter
            like gold
         on the cusp of
               worldly attachment,
            the golden deer
                  and
            the golden empire
                  are but
               a speck of Holy dust.

'x' AND 'n'
THE GRAMMAR OF RELATIONSHIP

In the all-encompassing
    darkness
    here
    there,
and everywhere
    even beyond.

'x' is the
beacon light
    the courage of
        hope
to move forward
    to a land of
    belonging
        and
     being
        of growing up
            there,
      from being
            to
        becoming.

Like my loving mother
　　　'x'
　　　　energises my
beak of
food gathering
　　　and
　　　　wings to fly,
　　　　　fly
　　　　　　beyond the clouds.

Then,
one stands alone
　　　one walks on a
　　　lonely road
　　　　to traverse paths
　　　　　　ahead.

'n'
illumines
　　　unfolds
　　　　the multi-hued possibilities
　　　　　　of seeds,
　　　　stored in my
　　　ancestral granary of
　　　　　Yore.
　　　　　Piercing the penumbra of
　　　　　　rainbow
　　　　　　　I
　　　　　　move to the
　　　　　　　Universe of Wisdom,
　　　　Cosmos of Consciousness
　　　　　　　　to get

the feel of
Divine Bliss.

'x'
the epitome of
  My Mother
     Put me
        in my known world of
          Belonging.

'n'
the replica of
    My Father
      inspires me
        to move
      on a wild spree
      to explore
        the possibilities
          of unknown.

THE SILENCE - - -
BETWEEN TWO WORDS

A silence
before
  the Great Explosion
  Eternity has its
      Image
  within itself.

The textual discourse of
    LIFE
  throughout,
    in Time and
    Timelessness
      narrates only
        two chapters
        'I'
        and
        'The other',
        with a
        foreword
        o n
          physical reality
            and
          Eternal silence,
         the two are
         complete
        unto themselves.

A line is
  drawn
    with potential possibilities of
        germination
         of
       Convergence
        and
       Divergence.

'We'
('I' and 'The other')
  chose ironically
     to be
    Ourselves
    in different
      dimensions.
     we did so
    on divergent deductions
       on the same core
     Theorem of
          what.....
          lies.....
          Beyond.....
Returned
  after sunset
    to the indivisible
     lap of mother,
    sucked the
  same breast
    converged
      on a point of
    Eternal Silence
      till

       the serpent of Tomorrow
           divided us into
              two separate
                selves,
           the seprent of
              uncertainty
                has
                  riches and power
                      on its hood.
The territory of
    Empire
    expanded
    upto
    infinity.
Carnal Pleasure
        o n
        The Throne
        distorted
        the stream of consciousness.
One fine morning
    on the
Summer Solstice
    a murmur
  alongwith the wind
  from the horizon
        resonates
    "A speck of
      celestial dust
        descends
          to this Earth
              to lose
            its identity.

BLACK EAGLE BOOKS

www.blackeaglebooks.org
info@blackeaglebooks.org

Black Eagle Books, an independent publisher, was founded as a nonprofit organization in April, 2019. It is our mission to connect and engage the Indian diaspora and the world at large with the best of works of world literature published on a collaborative platform, with special emphasis on foregrounding Contemporary Classics and New Writing.

www.ingramcontent.com/pod-product-compliance
Lightning Source LLC
Chambersburg PA
CBHW020539080526
44583CB00013B/919